S0-AVA-639

Received on

JUN 1 2 2019

Green Lake Library

EVERY RAVENING THING

NO LONGER PROPERTY
SEATTLE PUBLIC LIBRARY

PITT POETRY SERIES

Ed Ochester, Editor

EVERY RAVENING THING

MARSHA DE LA O

University of Pittsburgh Press

Published by the University of Pittsburgh Press, Pittsburgh, Pa., 15260
Copyright © 2019, Marsha de la O
All rights reserved
Manufactured in the United States of America
Printed on acid-free paper
10 9 8 7 6 5 4 3 2 1

ISBN 10: 0-8229-6575-5
ISBN 13: 978-0-8229-6575-6

Cover art: Nora Yukon, *The Dancer*
Cover design: Melissa Dias-Mandoly

for Estrella

CONTENTS

Interrogation   3
Poem of the first kiss   4
Keats at Fourteen   5
Darkfall   6
No, She Didn't Think the Road Was Dangerous   8
To Stand in a Circle   10
Two for a Penny   11
Gray Fox   12
Lament   13

Poem beginning in loneliness   17
My Vulture, My Companion   18
For the Poet Enheduanna of Uruk   23
La Vida   24
For a Young Woman Dead at Twenty   26
Vinegar of Roses   27
In the middle of the story   28
Ode to Apples   29

Speaking to my Father on War   33
Night Traveling   35
I Still Say Your Name   36
Running Fire   38
The Work of Their Hands   39
Ode to the Verb To Be   41
Self Portrait as Daphne   42
The Good Neighbor   45
In Those Months Gold Leaf Drifted onto His Skin   47

The Understory   51

Poem for the parched   52

Summer   53

A Natural History of Light   54

To Get This Far   56

Star Pine   57

The Essence of Water   59

Rio Grande   61

Bone Box   63

Mad Meg   67

Northern Lights and Sound   68

Mapping Hallucinations   69

Space-time Tsunami   70

The Country That Doesn't Exist   71

Poem on a female goldfinch   72

A Grove of Trees   73

Rough Innocence   76

Portion   77

To the Grandmothers   78

Acknowledgments   79

EVERY RAVENING THING

Interrogation

What plants do you harvest in the dark of the moon?
What bodies form halos?

Cinnamon, menth, and lavender.
                              Dandelions and dark matter,
the moon—
          cup overflowing
                                        broken harp
          punctured amulet shedding talc.

In this world, what did you see?
What shapes did light take?

Amber, and sheen of pearl.
                              Boneflower and weeping girl,
the moon—
          old woman's satchel
                                        saltlick
          shadowface in the well.

Can you say what you want?

To lay it down   lay my story down
    over the harm   like   a blanket of moth wings,

    Death's Head, Luna, White Witch,   I want
                                        to lay my story down.

Poem of the first kiss

The water in the spillway was only that, water, I understood the weight of water with its load of silt, I understood silt, the burden of carrying and letting go, the idea of a trench, the idea of encasing a watercourse in concrete, they released me in late afternoon in the season of early dark, a strained light still shone, three little words, oh please,   please, I'm not a girl like others now, ordinary in ordinary light, the djinn ended that, the djinn lit down and smacked me good, crossing the bridge, water in the spillway only water, late afternoon moon, leaves green and breathing, I hear their little sighs, enough rain fallen the week before to wake the dead, that lily that knew to renounce every green thing and wait, clenched and knotted, that lily understood stay dead, play dead, but couldn't resist in the end; much later I'll live in another country, and there will be book clubs, and one woman will tell the story of how it happened in the fifth grade at the first Star Wars movie, her fingers brushing the silk of his cheek and she still knows his name, and my turn is coming, I'm waiting, getting ready to look nobody in the face, and say, *I don't remember.*

Keats at Fourteen

She dozes, her nails fretted against the linen's border,
a hectic rose flaming each cheek. Her lips move, no words.
The boy is guardian spirit, no one but he enters this sickroom
where his mother fades, home finally after six years—failures,
disgrace. *Scarlet daughter,* neighbors hiss, *slave to appetite,*
but John is single-minded—she *will* live. No one but he gives her
the tincture of mercury—one tenth of a grain daily, dabs the sweat
of her fevers away, a basket of withered poppies at his feet. He pierces
each capsule with a needle, drops it in a small glazed crock to warm
near the stove, sweat out the opium. Then he'll add wine, saffron,
nutmeg. It takes time, the hour darkens. He cups his hand
to light the votive. She moans a furred voice from webbed lungs,
a cup of black blood brimming, *the pilgrim is fleeing the City,*
he leans in closer, *the City of Destruction,* takes her clammy hand,
that place also where he was born, so close now he's breathing her,
"Johnny," she cries, "lift me up, Johnny, your father is here in the room."

Darkfall

Because black blood beat against his temples

                                     like muffled wings and
there was never a moment when he
                didn't feel that trembling, and because

that same blood flowed slowly
                    over the stone of his skull as he paced, stopped,

and looked around; *I served my country,* he'd say in a hurt,
        bewildered voice, like he still couldn't believe it.

Because Vietnam followed him home
                      in a beat of black blood, always
a bank of heavy light.

Because every darkfall ripened into nightmare
                       & overwhelmed—he could not

          change it into anything else, and could not
stop it, and neither one of us thought
          to wonder if we believed in love—we did not—
and because he could not
        believe in sleep, the dream came to dwell in daylight.

He was infantry and I was high school, I lay around
                   smoking his dope, nervous
because he never made a move on me,
          but grateful too, that it wasn't compulsory,
he wanted nothing so much
          as to smoke and talk in a flat voice
      while I sat,
         head propped against the wall, body
shanked on a stained mattress.

Because he spelled his name *Ric* without the *k*,
            and once we might've been friends.

Because he sometimes disappeared
                    and the dream did all the talking,
          coming into being
and he suffered alone in that empty room
                              where I was nothing.

Only a body of silence
               the dream moved through.
          Only a hand
                holding a joint, letting smoke rise.

Because they were coming, they were always coming
                                        through trees
into a shoal of light, and he could see the way
                light pounded heat into thick air,

and there was never any wind.

The Viet Cong ride on grasshoppers
                                through the dark trees,
perched up high on huge grasshoppers
                with bodies like moving scaffolds,

and here's the thing he couldn't get past:
                     their eyes, enormous and deep,
          like the eyes of horses
whose muzzles he'd stroked,
                     that pure,

and tears brim up in their eyes
                and fill to overflowing
          and trace a wet shining.

Against those tears, all weapons are useless.

No, She Didn't Think the Road Was Dangerous

Eastern Congo

she walked that road every day,
the aid worker translates for the stranger—

Faida bending in the peanut field, muscles
warming and stretching, silk of sweat
at the nape of her neck,

then the two hour trudge to market at Minova
with peanuts in a sack on her back,
thinking only of her return with firewood.

She met the soldiers in the afternoon,
hardly more than boys, whether Mai-Mai
or Hutu she never knew.

One boy wore a Nike tee and smiled
when he said *you can choose life,
or death.* She tried to run. Here,

she looks up, her eyes beseech
the journalist, he forces
himself not to look away—

so heavy my load,
she shakes her head,
the same road I always took,

here, the story breaks down,
she holds an envelope in her hand,
a letter from her husband—

her exile followed,
moving lost through fields
of manioc, down red clay paths

thirty miles to tin-roofed Goma,
baby in a sling on her hip—
she takes out a single sheet

folded in thirds, covered in script,
small hoard of invaders, jointed
legs, segmented bodies,

a sudden burst of rain
beats down, street filling, words
boil forth like a nest of ants,

and the words swim—she cannot read
the words and the journalist cannot
read the words—and the rain pounds

and the water shouts *you are cast out,
you have no home.* He's quiet,
typing into his phone—

she's two inches in a piece on rare
earth, one out of a quarter million,
a beggar, a statistic, her name is Faida—

and the baby sobs, Faida bends
to the glassy dark of his eyes, *O little one,
hush; hush now thy lamentations.*

To Stand in a Circle

Drums draw me down in sunlight
        at noon to the plaza, and there—
women in homemade black shifts as though
        they'd torn and dyed their sheets.
One woman carries a wreath of gladiolus,
        her face smeared with ash.
Hard to make out a bullhorn's static and bray,
        first in Catalan and then Castilian—
street theater against rape in Bosnia, in Spain,
        suicide swims out of the pounding,
murder slips out of the garble. Hard light,
        thick as topaz. My broken Spanish
and urge to escape. To be human is to stand
        in a circle. The woman with the black mouth
steps to the center. Speaking to no one
        from somewhere inside an iron sorrow,
Mija, she cries, raft of flowers at her feet, her voice
        the mineral that flew into fire
calling a daughter gone to earth, *mija*, her voice
        a bird, delicate fretwork of feather
and bone lit up in lineament of flame, and flame
        itself turns to wings. When it's over,
when she weeps, when words no longer serve,
        when I finally leave, her voice stays
with me, crouched inside my ear, stays as I trudge
        up the sixty-three steps to my flat.
What can you do with a voice like that?
        I stow it in a velvet bag carried across an ocean
along with the light on cathedral stone. I carry it here.
        And what is a voice, really? Nothing,
but a bloody string. And a vibration. And silence.

Two for a Penny

She'd locked the door and somehow lost the key   a faulty keychain   hadn't she
told him   and the spare nearby   After so long without rain   sparrows fought to
bathe in the dust   *take a moment wait*   Falling she had time to wonder why   the
freight of drink   of the past   her shoes   her absurd pumps   the weight of an entire
body balanced on two slender sticks   She'd locked the door and somehow lost
the key   Falling she had time to wonder   the slightest breeze   a small rush of
wings   could've toppled her   the man upright   woman prone   but it wasn't the
wind   By now we've gone beyond the gloaming   we're losing light   He
struck her   Falling she had time   How small she is beneath his sway   In the
Bible sparrows are two for a penny   but never apart from the Father   These
lovers   this slippage   loving every ravening thing   salt of their kisses   salt sting
an errant tooth gashed her lip   and here's providence   something broke her fall
her new stepchildren never saw *wait*   After so long without rain   dirt becomes
a kind of silk   *slow down and breathe*   sparrows battle one another to bathe   in
a dustshaft   She toppled   A small king beating his wings against the ground
dust rising like talcum   a rush of wings   the jacaranda   a crowned sparrow
hush now   Her head empty   a few stars like a handful of salt scattered on a map
of nothing   Sometimes on your back   you actually feel the world spinning   all
the shame   The children knew to disappear   his babies could hide on a dime
Jacaranda   blossoms petalling the patio   violet gone gray   *try this start over
it doesn't make sense*

Gray Fox

Years later on the headlands, chevrons
of seed stalks brim with light, midsummer
in a parched year, feral tang of eucalyptus,
walking slowly, scanning for her coat
of ash and gold in an arid field, the neat
triangle of her face, so long I've known
this animal, since my daughter was a child
and first saw her, stretched out an arm
to the dark-rimmed eyes holding our gaze,
afternoon flecked with summer ending,
she's a drift of gold in dry air, topaz
of her stare regarding us, stopping time,
that moment carried with me since, leaf shadow,
mottled shade now disappearing into . . .
now vanishing, but *here* this whole way
on the other side, her sharp face, time past
and time to come, hope like electricity
in a cloud, that this wildness should last.
That she holds on. That she found a way
to pass life through her.

Lament

For Philip Levine

The wisteria disappeared early this year,
blown out by merciless wind you called the *Levante*,
trees shuddering, wind tearing at the ruined sea.
Like you, I travelled to live in a village in
Spain, mornings I watched Gypsy day-laborers
on the corner waiting for flat-bed trucks
in their thin jackets, and in the evening
the tiny figure of the flower-seller with
her bundles trudging the length of Calle
Madrid. The *Levante* swept over the red butte
down deep cuts toward the village, battered
our faces, our hearts. One relentless morning
I pried off my wedding ring, left my family,
and bought a ticket at the Valencia *Estacion
del Nord*. I remember rusting autos in ravines
as we left the city, a broken-open emptiness
in my chest that might have been possibility,
wind punishing the silver-backed leaves of
the olive trees. *If you wait long enough,
the wind answers itself,* didn't you say that?
The train strained up a grade towards a white
village. A magpie swooped over stubble
in the fields. The wait wasn't long—the wind died.
I looked out, and saw storks nesting on rooftops,
on high balustrades, the brushwork of their nests
large enough for a child, an eight-year-old—
like my daughter, her gangly legs outpacing her,
my stork-child. The air grew calm. I shoved
the ring back over the knuckle of my third
finger and got off at the next stop. The only
answer to death is love. *Caballero,* you
have gone into the hard earth of your
valley, the great mountains brooding in
the east, our Sierras, their relentless grinding,
slip, and sudden thrust upward, outward,
our broken-hearted California.

Poem beginning in loneliness

        Let's start
with the loneliness
              of beauty
                  o human
in this mottled world
        how deep and cold
the standing stone
            and sweet the light
        warming its flank

and all the earth breathing

        the stream snappy
as lion cubs tangling
with small guttural roars and swipes
        tumbling
over rocks

        the moon a sow
            lolling
                on her side

and the sun ____   beyond words
        blind one   furnace
who started all this

        and still
           I want   I want

My Vulture, My Companion

i
Captives

At the side of the road, a stand that sold
dark grapes, and summer's last sweet corn, and
behind, a tangle of scrub oak and maple,
leaves already burning down to gold,
letting go, spiral-flung, dancing imps
of wind as we pass.
     We would not stop there, I knew.
The trees hold themselves up in their world
and our world is behind the glass.
What a couple of henny-pennies, not just
afraid, ashamed . . . we'd been tricked and I'd taken
a hit, and now I can't think.
        All afternoon
daylight flows through a crack in the window.

You're thirteen-year-old-runaways. We tell them
we're seventeen, but they want younger girls.

ii
Lilies of the Field

"We're down in the dirt," they say, "and
you're lilies of the field. The field is full
of cowshit, girls." Daylight flows through a crack
in the window. The men wear long knives

in leather holsters, blades nestled in sheaths,
sheaths resting on blue-jeaned thighs.
In the distance a vulture circles slowly,
dark form suffused with light, silence

                          ascending,

bird suspending above the gray-blue
sea, above the mountain's burnish,
wide sail of his wings tilting slightly

one way, then another. I want this bird
to stop time, my companion, my vulture.
I want the ride to last, I want the light to hold.

iii
Saffron

Light won't hold, light pours through glass.
October here is dust, is saffron, a stun-rod
of drought; empty seedheads of wild grass,
lit spindles. This window hurts so much
it screams when I roll it down.
                                    Her inscription:
for my daughter, who loves light as
                did the Greeks of olden days,
her careful penmanship, her careless child.

And here's Eurydice with a python
round her neck, *cool headgear,* she cries,
                                    all stoned,
(now there's a lonely haunt).
                                    Orpheus is riding
shotgun, big raw hands resting on his knees,

he smiles, "You'd do anything to stay alive, right?'
What a fucking cliché. No possible answer.
                                    (either way)

iv
Cloaked by Wings

An immense bridge disappearing into fog.
No way to say how you enter the city

                                        a prisoner.

Not possible. The golden shoulders of hills
above the clouds of Marin. No answer

                                to the white

city swept clean, the white city shaping itself
in each of us, alone. No possible way. The mind
is cloaked by wings. "Girls, we're in the Mission. If
we let you out here, in thirty seconds a black man

would have you up in his room."

                                We're supposed to
be scared of that when we're trapped with them?
One of us cries, "I'll take him! I'd take anyone!

But you! Because WHO WOULD EVER WANT YOU!
A beat of silence and the shouting starts.   One of us
spoke the last sentence many girls ever get to say.

v

A Pair of Shoes

How do you ever *really* get away? One blond, one dark,
one punished, one not. After, we burned and shivered
until there was nothing left to say.
                              Whatever your name is
now—surely not still Buffy—in the long journey

away from that day, I took the serrated wings.
I didn't take you, and you didn't keep me.
                                   Oh Sharon,
oh Helen, with your golden ramparts of hair,
                                       what is poetry
that refuses to remember—a pair of shoes that runs

for years . . . serrated wings . . . ?
                        Suppose some evening we met,
lifted our eyes across the aisle
                 in the dark tunnel—
                              they punished
us both, Sharon, do you remember how
                              changed we were,

and could not tell?
                        He folds a five dollar bill and
slips it into your hand when they pull the car
onto the dirt and
                       let us out at the side of the road.

For the Poet Enheduanna of Uruk

2350 B.C

She considers the shape of an idea. That lightning resembles a feather. The poet presses her wedge-shaped reed into soft red clay. A shaft and slender barbs, this reed plucked from the banks of the Tigris and cut into a stylus. Tigris Sunrise is one of her names. Her name as color and motion. Her liquid name. Cloudscapes release their charge with a strike. A shaft and feathering. Lightning and feather. Same symbol for both, line and cross-hatching, small flag in strong wind. Her name as light. A corona forms around the central shaft. A tree reaches upward to call lightning down. A night enfeathered with storm, darkness split with branching light. When Uruk fell, her temple destroyed, Lugalanne the conqueror, defiled her. Always she remembers the little pouch his fish-lips made as they parted and came together before he smiled. She considers the word's weight. A narrow gorge. A ruined heart. Lightning is not ethereal. Even a feathery corona smashes against a roof like a load of sunbaked clay. He keeps her alive, but why? That people might witness her debasement, his trophy. He keeps her alive. She considers lightning and feathers. The charge enters at the nape of her neck and flows downward like water. Her limbs start up in a concord of fire and water and her hand picks up the stylus, this chance to sing back the world—this is how an exile returns to the city. The poet presses her wedge-shaped reed into soft red clay.   She inscribes her name. *Nin-me-sar-ra.*

La Vida

Barcelona, 1995

He's a boy all in black

as though his mother were a raven,
black cap of hair, huge leather jacket,

wisp of cigarette smoke, eye of flame.
Dust floats the gold in autumn air,

light in every cell. Behind him,
anarchists protest a new law—

la policia now free to seize their flutes
and drums, to steal their chalk.

Boys in boots kneel on the sidewalk,
scrawling quick obscene drawings

while their brothers pound on drums
and shriek through little flutes.

Raven boy shoves a leaflet in my hand.
Everyone has a right to work! If we're treated

like criminals, we might be forced to turn to ROBBERY.

There is no work here. They're work-orphans,
Father Work abandoned them

and hopped a bus across the border.
A small wind dissolves the afternoon,

grains of dust swim inside the light.
They must be motes of silence—

no one remembers what happened to anarchists.

The boy holds out his palm for pesetas.
He's a flurry of air, a rippling,

quicksilver face—stipple of dark
hair across his upper lip,

enough of the child left
to discern the child he was,

slender, taller than me—
life pressing against time,

sheen of iridescence, and moving on.

Standing, facing him, I can feel the earth
beneath the stones of the plaza;

I give him all the silver I've got.

For a Young Woman Dead at Twenty

She liked to slow-walk, heat-held, alone in groves behind the dorm
a sultry September night, lonely girl,
green-growing inside, tongue-tied in English class.

All those tongues tolling the bell, the knell, the gong: gone . . . gone . . . gone.
All that speculation, yawp and pang,
those letters home to our parents.

I keep my mouth shut, but the pang hammers away like a clock
wrapped around 3 sticks of dynamite,
heart sprocketed, wheels engaged.

To walk alone at night for sweet relief
when heat clamps us in a vise,
they warn us to never.

I'm all haywire, blast-bound, rocked:
another trashcan fire, another girl defaced, defrocked,
and then comes grief.

Her name is Lois.

Vinegar of Roses

Blue Ridge, 1810

Child, I remember carrying your small
body over frozen ground the morning
after the full moon, tightly wound in
muslin, winter ivory, my eyes fiercely
dry as though I could no longer weep.
You were perfectly empty, immaculate
as sky, one shade of gray. But what
does air have to do with me? As winter
trapped us under the cloud's linen, as
winter wrapped the moon in bandages,
black bile rose even unto my throat
for I was ever of a singular element—
earth alone. Alone the greater part
of February—snow fell and carried
me through days submerged in no-
time, death a crow shadow on snow.
And now, boughs of our white pines
settle against the air, sway and settle,
whispering hushed sounds. The earth
softens enough to bury a body. Pitch
brightens the pines' bark, a salve for
wounds, that pitch, if you have healing
hands: my hands wrung the cloth and
smoothed the petals onto your brow,
Child, Roses of Castile, dark blooms
steeped in brine—Vinegar of Roses.
I tore the blossoms apart myself.
You were all I had. I would've burnt
down the house, scorched the fields
if I thought it would open your eyes.

In the middle of the story

She knows a kestrel pair lives somewhere near
the abandoned barn where she meets her son's
angry father and they pass their boy from her car
to his, and when she arrived a few minutes early
she stood outside and listened for the small
burst of their cries, *cree cree*—this morning,
only silence—then caught a glint of light by
the side of the road, her polished beak—the female
had been hit. The kestrel cradled in her hands,
speckled-salmon breast still soft, wings of muted-
slate, she's part of it now—the bird's hush and
sheen. She'll always heed the way light opens
on this stretch of road, listen for their ratcheting call
turning the day in one direction only, beak and talons
ripping flesh and she's part of that, she's windhover,
blue-gray dimensions, ultraviolet—for the first
time she can see the bright and disappearing trail.
How deep the quiet carries her. Now what will
the male do? In three days, she'll be back to get her boy.

Ode to Apples

Chinese lanterns in the leaves, globes
            of springwater drawing me in,
fistful of radiance:

what glistens is golden
                        Delicious, satin
Gala, Winesap, a bare
room of snow in a little red dress,

                        Magdalene, crimson
as the dark queen's mouth. Done
with the tango of sugar and light
                        spun into flesh

pure circlets of force, they wait
for the wind to rise.   Around here,
a wicker basket's easy to find

laden with hand-sized burgundy mirrors
                        spackled in stars.
Take one. Peer into your life. Why not
 pray to what's rooted in earth:

Apples of Autumn,
                        let me plummet
into your charmed windfall,

let me bless, finally, the snake—

oh lil' darling, redhead, my struck match—
before the leaves
            are driven from the trees.

Speaking to my Father on War

You and I never
spoke much
you kept the radio on
in the pickup

the talk jock going
on about whatever
the darkness
of the day was.

I learned to love
the empty places
without you,
the warehouse after

you'd gone out
on your delivery route.
And what we've come
to finally, is this

prodigal silence
whose distance can't
be calibrated.
At seventeen you

work for your father
because he needs you,
and after his death,
because he needed you.

You work with glass.
Your hands bleed.
Everything that comes
to you is broken.

I came to you.
To a child, the logic
is irrefutable. Now I
want to posit that war

is a rebuke
to the transformative
power of language.
They say that words

can't bear that weight.
You have your implements
torch, wrench, saw tooth
blade. The heat of your will.

Night Traveling

I'm a grown woman, and know Buddhist scripture
makes no distinction between beauty and ugliness
in the Pure Land. My dreams are not that land.

The story never changes. Always in a car. Those
pilgrim girls, this painful impermanent earth,
a sutra is a thread that holds things together.

I do miss a good night's sleep, don't you?

When Milosz says, *what reasonable man would
like to be a city of demons,* I choose to believe
he includes woman in the word 'man'.

I drive through imperial night. The thread is ugliness.
You must know how power fails to make us safe, those
prisons for mothers and children built on the border.

The moon threads her needle through my eyes, lashes
them open. Here come the cars with trapped girls:

they're too young, barely speak the language, not sure
what *put out or get out* means, they press their palms
against the side windows, each one crying *I'll get out.*

I Still Say Your Name

even though you finally
blew the roof off this place
and flew away over highways
and housetops into yonder—

maybe there's no drum machines
where you're at, maybe there's stacks
of garages, a warren, a whole city,
and a band's tuning up in each one:

an empty place at the drum set,
a kit with a missing man—slide
into your seat, touch sticks to skin,
the bass player picks up the rhythm   easy

all of you swinging into it,
by now you got your boogaloo,
by now your mojo's working, sound going
down like velvet, like whiskey.

Go on,
play the tune about hope.
Close your eyes,

play the dark where music comes from
that tune so perishing sweet
that tune where wings
brush your face

and when you open your eyes
you're at the river,
young and strong again,
sticks in your hand going like magic.

Now play one for us back here,
a little song of remembrance,
play the one about the man
who came home with a shepherd

pup, one last thing to love
before quitting this world, one last
love to share, and how that dog
sang for hours the morning after.

Running Fire

After the explosion I couldn't understand why God   *Like a*
would do such a thing—a dirt road even the dogs deserted,   *sheep-child*
          and I wake up an empty sleeve,   *wedged inside*
    a mason jar,

caught a glimpse of what looked like a length of round steak   *like a mandrake*
before they strapped me down—no pain, only pity and wonder—   *wrapped in*
          my poor arm, my mouth whispered,   *batting,*

nerves a smear of bloody threads just hanging   *like a*
after they severed the mangle, but my doctor tells me,   *pig-iron pothook*
No, Ms. Kit,   *without*
          dangling telephone wires—he's mechanical-minded,   *a skillet,*

though I know a few things—one divides into two,   *like a*
absence and phantom, and you can't stop   *floating*
a phantom from coming back,   *ghost*
          she knows what happened.   *lantern,*

It's all fire in the stump,   *like the*
brain fire, running fire, spiring up, *electrical*   *blue-veined*
storm, Doc Miller says, and when my face furrows,   *shine*
he promises, *one of these*   *inside*
          is the Rosetta Flame, Ms. Kit.   *a blaze,*

                           Last month   *like*
he took an awl and pierced my shoulder for his itty-bitty   *an exile*
motherboard, *let's see if we can get those fires built*   *humping*
in the clearing, and though trouble   *her life*
          and shadow tweak their guy-lines,   *on her back,*

still these nerves go on working,   *like*
and when he says *turn your hand, palm in:*   *a head*
imagine that motion, and the phantom is with you,   *on a pike,*

and we hear, both of us, the soft whisper   *I*
of the electric motor on the artificial limb   *remember*
          as she turns my hand, palm in.   *everything.*

The Work of Their Hands

The old cemetery's shaved green,
an entire hillside, flank and shoulders,

grassy smell and high black fence,
a row of iron spikes, barbed to catch and hold.

The air is full of vapors as if memory churns

up mist, and just below, the road with its crest
and drop—a lure for boys driving at speed

enough to enter air caged inside a metal box.

The boys want their fun, to shrug off
the weight of our quiet hill.

A body gives up its poor secret easily.

And, yes, they want to shrug off the work
of their hands, this thing they began

and can't get free of,

it started almost as a laugh, but the radio
urges them on, all the voices inside a song

they won't stop shouting or singing.
The words are arrows for the heart, arrows

that pierce, barbed to catch and hold
the heart-muscle sutured with iron spikes.

The heart does not let go its wound.

Will they be able to put this away
with other things best forgotten?

And her face so tightly closed she might
have been a doll. And how small she is,

they paused to wonder.

And the straight skirt I, her mother, made,
a gingham check in yellow and white,

oh, surely, my girl is cured of gingham.

Ode to the Verb To Be

I sit in the car next to his red mouth
and flushed face. Whipping my head
around. The sky is green as copper. Two
arms twist to hold the legs. One mouth
sings Blueberry Hill. The bear came
to the mountain at the same time as Sal—
she with a bucket, he with the shovel
of his paw. The bear lolls in the sun,
huge arms spread wide. He's laughing.
I'm in my blood mask, my briar. Some-
times I see the sky through her, carbon
blue, she can't talk—her voice is trapped
in a warehouse fire, her voice is lost
in a city of teeth. We're always looking
for the right way to wear disgrace,
my mother sewed an entire suit
on her Singer but couldn't make it
fit, she didn't know zip how to clothe
an echo—that mute who disappeared
in the forest, her molecules are smaller
than the wavelengths of light. I helped
her run for it, but I had to stay. Some-
times you can just make out a shape
in the eyes of girls, hidden, the way
rage is covered by calm; calm is a husk,
rage is a region of excited electrons.
I grow taller, my mother calls me in
to stand on a stool and pins up the hem
of the dress. There's heat all around
escaping my corona. I'm in my blood
mask, my briar. Who could bear her hands
brushing private flames? I know I can't.

Self Portrait as Daphne

How did you get in this little room?
    Window propped partway open,
Gayla sitting in her underpants on the closed
    toilet expertly planting a needle in her thigh.
A dog barks somewhere outside.

You can't tear your eyes away from that syringe—
    does poison grow stronger
for passing through the mind's eye?
    And if my thoughts have wronged her?
Oh, look away, look away into walls . . .

not too-too solid here, some atomic breath
    plumps and slacks them, rose-
colored walls rising and falling, ah porcelain,
    ah buzzing particulars,
Gayla my mirror, needle-in-the-vein-Gayla.

You want out but which way is out?
    And thinking like the roar of a train.
What do you know about truth?
    For you, being wrong altogether is
First Cause. Is Gayla that kind of girl?

Wrong thoughts break vessels, wrong
    thoughts cause blood leaks.
Pay attention!   Concentrate
    on the numbers: one to turn about,
three down the hall, six to the door,

and by declension come—to a mirror,
    ms small- and-dark, ms animal-nature,
can barely lift her eyeshafts,
    and if my thoughts have wronged her?
Quick, get away, get out of here,

but can you run from him? Kingpin, Sultan?
    Johnny, (is that his name)
with both arms spread like wings
    on the velvet settee, opens and
closes his mouth. No words.

Johnny-on-the-sofa, pocket-full-of-radium.
    And if he means you harm, so must
you flee. Now she steals out the door
    and it's off to the races, *thud* of her Vans
on the sidewalk, cars slamming by,

migrating electrical wallop passing
    from eggshell blue to blanch, the world's
not solid—dust of particles, empty space—
    then left onto Verdugo Road,
running slower now, breath burning,

from weakness to lightness and by
    declension   come to pieces.
There's tricks in the world. Trees
    full of milk, leaves silver
on the blade edge,

tell me, why am I alive?
    Trees wave their thousand knives.
Now a black dog noses a branch
    at the corner of Verdugo and Adams
and everything depends on him.

The trees are bleeding milk—
    do you want to get home,
burst through the kitchen door,
    startled mother at the sink
or is it better never to go back—

knives in the air already slicing
   she pounds toward the black dog.
If his eyes are yellow
   and meet mine, *thine evermore,*
as long as I keep breathing.

The dog lifts his muzzle,
   those eyes—gold-flecked,
and now what will god do—
   oh please— change my form,
whence all my sorrows come.

The Good Neighbor

Maybe he'd always kept an eye on me because when I felt well enough
to stand out front in a shaft of thin sun, he came right over

and I confessed I'd been sick. *What about food*, he asked,
No problem, thinking of a whole line of Campbell's lentil-whatever

like dumb soldiers waiting by the stove, *I got canned soup,*
and if you dump in cold rice, it really holds you.

Two hours later he stood at the door with a pot of chicken and dumplings.

Then *he* was the one who disappeared, at least three months, gone,
his band never practiced, finally, after Christmas, I glimpsed his face

through branches of the olive
something puzzling about his skin, a different shine,

we met on the sidewalk, his eyes huge, full
of glistening yellow threads,

legs nearly wasted away, no tissue left—*Good god, Dave, what?*

You know, he said, *I always thought I'd die in Vietnam,*
and then I thought I'd die young right here, and then I got sober.

He shrugged, *Hep C, stage 4 cirrhosis.*
Poison already everywhere. The blood slowed, tide swelling

an inland sea. He turned his palms up. *But the thing is,*
everybody has Hep C. I thought, whole legions, battalions,

and maybe we should have embraced right then, but all I did
was repeat his words staggered back to him,

Yeah, everyone has Hep C, and then we were quiet
and he shook his head.

Didn't much care he couldn't take in food, just carried the hope

he'd grow strong enough to play again, which was the null set,
already he'd lost his home in the rhythm, the beat coming undone

thump by thump until he understood how hope turns us into fools.
And maybe they were dumb, those legions of young men,

those foolish battalions, but it's not hard to imagine
how you could share your kit with your buddies,

slamming it all together, let the sweet slurry of the rush smack
into each one of you, steal over the dark, over the salt

of stars above, and everywhere around you, the war.

In Those Months Gold Leaf Drifted onto His Skin

Late nights, late nights, rain fingered his guitar,
He played bars every weekend, trained dogs
on the side, dreamed an orchard out back,
white peaches, dark plums.
                              Once he made a barbecue
from a fifty-gallon drum, simmered mussels
in wine.
                              Late nights, late nights,
talking through winter, his laugh turned to velvet
when the temperature dropped.

Scorpion on his bicep, at his heels an Alsatian.
All through summer his garden spoke in tongues,
stone fruit, dark plums.
                              The day they told him *no,*
not a chance for a transplant, he took a whisk
broom to the cemetery, swept his father's grave.

Dark nights, dark nights, rain pierced his eyes.
When the Feather River overtopped its banks
he finally got down
                              to the slow work of drowning.

The Understory

Through this window, the way she is
without me in the sycamore, fox squirrel
descending to the understory, quick
and timorous, deep of eye, small
muscled forepaws.
       Past morning now at my bare
white table, a window opening onto
the world and finally a squirrel arrives—
unfurling her motile tail with a flourish,
that mutable organ, fleur-de-lys, ash-
gold plume, peacock's broom, lightning
play of neurons in a pleasure burst—
what could this shapeshifter want?
             I remember how
you told me once with your eyes what
you wanted, and I understood instantly—
that way of knowing so entire.
             Sea fog
in the gum trees, autumn sun steeped
in vatic mist. Dream-leaf among the
quantum on the asphalt.
             And I knew
 at once, too, the moment I was banished,
though we lay together another season.
             How sleek
my squirrel in russet and gray—
is it curiosity that leads her to pick up
a fallen sycamore leaf, pummel it with
her paws and carry it away?
             What are you
doing, little mother, what could you want
with that leaf?
          The wind nudges the door
shut behind me, reticent wind, quiet as
some wild thing, glimpsed
           and vanishing.

Poem for the parched

Oak gall, bay berry,
silver wool of santanilla,
no one knows how I thirst
toyon, aloe, weeping leaves
of the pepper tree.

Summer

As far south as possible—to live—the ache
on the edge of what can't be endured,
Monterey cypress on the spit, this remnant.

When will longing be done with me:

parched, parched St. Catherine's Lace
fuming her last, and Sister Datura,
mi loca, my girl, her closed mouth

twisted like paper, horses in the shallows,
piebald and panicked, rearing
in the foam, ghost eyes wide, oh far-

ranging roans, blue multitudes
rushing the horizon—*why oh why can't I*—
naturally I dream the length of summer

days & nights when the moon
lives for weeks in my room,
staggering in late every night drunk,

slip sliding off her shoulders
into an ivory pool on the carpet,
and still, she will not ease me.

A Natural History of Light

I

A small bird cries *could-be, could-be,* above my head, mousy little thing,
one of those drab gray birds in this dry land, December sun streaming
in low, December rain jostling the arroyo.
                          could-be, could-be calls Drab Gray.

Our universe, physicists say, is a cosmological relic—
a glass ark with hammered gold seams, pip trapped inside, god's
knucklebone, nanosecond high-energy outward burst—ka-boom!—

and space fills up with proto-stars. I crouch at the edge of the arroyo.
Wind strokes my hand with its map of rivers.

O helium, lithium, hydrogen, you comfort me, o carbon, you are my flesh and bone.

II

Here on the river's verge, I could be busy for months without changing my place,
    simply
leaning a bit more to right or left. So says Cezanne. And now the sun leans
west like Cezanne, striking a rippling mirror of water
                              refracting into a mirror of granite.

Light pouring into matter; let us praise their equivalence, if only my mind
didn't flicker so— how you interpolate, my complicated friend, suddenly back
in touch. Ah, gray bird, do you ever get confused?
                       And the theorem that what is lost is lost?

Light shining on water's skin, flowing tremors . . .

III

Color is the place where our brain and the universe meet. And what would Cezanne
make of this verge—oakgold water, riverstones, wet, tawny leaves
and this impossible shade of deep and jade where water
slides over the shadow of a tree trunk,
                    runneling body of darkness, is it *sable-green?*

And the universe of patterns on granite—light as lattice, lacework, loose
weave, a dress knit of light Madame Cezanne wears, skein unraveling,
nakedness inside—bedazzlement— his complicated friend—

> he loved best
>
> > light's long kiss,
>
> > > light's ripple, unruly, water unspooling, spooling

down from the mountain, threads weaving together,

> > > coming undone . . .

And the theorem that nothing is lost?

IV

We are, Cezanne reminds me, *an iridescent chaos.* And perhaps he speaks of the nature
of light, or the coils in my mind, or

> Hortense with her hair loosened, alone, Hortense implacable in
> red, his family would not receive her, she bore his only son, raised him
> living apart, desperate for funds, they judged her, surface and depth, light
> on watered silk, how carefully she composed her pain
> through all those hours, all those portraits, twenty-nine of them,
> how marriage confounded them both, confounds us,

> > > > every

marriage

> spanning a ravine of time
>
> > down

in the canyon where stream and light and stone are one

> > flame,

yes, fire ascendant in water, fire paramount,

> > water catamount,

puma water, plum-colored in its darker parts . . .
I hear somewhere close

> that bird calling *could-be, could-be—*

tell me, Bird, how soul inhabits the place of fire,

> how soul dwells there in its trembling?

To Get This Far

The wind—stringent,

shoving me in the chest

every afternoon I exist.

I've travelled for years to get this far, the world

serving wind from tilled fields.

Now the sit-down, brewing the pot,

old words between us,

lifting a cup   not disenchanted

rueful,   a small whip in forgiveness,

we're grown up, we're sorry.

Tea is warmed-over wind,

spent cask, dried leaves

bodies sleeping—

creatures from our smaller kingdoms,

those sunlit moths, their gauzy

linen wings—

we still see a few—

the female lays her single egg

on the underside of mustard.

Star Pine

Time can slow to a halt in a hallway
with a view of a star-pine
by the pharmacy, and the roof below
with its carpet of asphalt and small rocks.
I've got a window seat and minor piety,
I've got a chant, thrumming:
        You, my faith, my ark, my bricks and mortar.
We've already said good-bye.

My rule is: keep your mouth shut.
We don't know how it gets in a body.
If I yawned, a tumor could flit inside
about the size of a cream puff or a golf ball
without symmetry—spikes and folds and webs
like a baby dragon.

And when it hatched, the mother
bent her fearsome neck
and moved that nestling
near where your blood bustles.

I've got a thick skull of hope
unwinding a vision, a picture
for afterwards:
you're pink-faced and twinkling, rosy-all-over,
maybe shambling a little, but otherwise
the same.
You're looking good.

I'm the life form with a sour smell.
It's fear, but I tell myself that's covered here
by the dead smell of food from the rolling carts.
The nurses smell of caution, they're non-committal.
They pad by in booties and hairnets, careful
of the I.V., the pole, the whole awkward procession,
a movable bed, a bag of clear liquid
dripping like mercy.

And the patients
with sheets drawn up to their chins
have suffered themselves to be tethered and pressed
like good and sweet animals.

The elevator opens, they're pushed inside,
the door closes behind them.
I watch them leaving, and wait for you.
The star pine leans toward the glass.
I'm mouthing thank you
and whispering please.

That star pine is your lost sister.
That star pine is your brother's soul,
sane and calm and cleansed.

The dragon
bends her fearsome neck;
the tree
is breathing next to the window.

Let it breathe for you.

The Essence of Water

A dove calls, turning its small motor over,
                                          and over again,
late July, a grove of California live oaks—
the old weavers spin their sugar, luff out oxygen,

light falling through beveled leaves
onto leaves below, something like presence
rustling in the silence.

All creatures know to stay still, hoping to hold onto their one life.

If I had to do it all over again, beginning
with a true reckoning, would fear be torn out by its roots?

And now, wind: invisible stream flowing east, one quantity
contained in another, the lungs of the Pacific
breathing out in afternoon, jangling sunlight,

each leaf a transparency; each leaf a prism.

The Upanishads say, "the essence of all beings
is the earth, the essence of earth is water,
and the essence of water is the tree."

Above the trunks and spreading limbs,
soft spheres of lit moisture, finespun,
the hours reworking their boundaries.

If we could let their equivalence
move through our bodies, surely, we
would know something of their quietude.

What would be enough to enter the peace of oaks?

It takes so much trust to walk out alone
contained in otherness, to let dusk fill the valley
and overflow the hilltops, to step into

a thousandfold of leaves, light slipping away,
wavering, shadows floating in air.

And I want this courage, I want
to walk alone at night
beneath the skirts of leaves and reach up

to touch the hem, just close enough,
as darkness sharpens the moon's golden knife
and wind stirs pianissimo in the crown,

each leaf must be a syllable of permission,
a way to say yes—let touch teach me.

Rio Grande

Susan at the barbecue
grilling squash and corn
while Amalio takes us
down to the river
the Navajo call
Female Waters
tumbling south.
Light-dazzled golden-
eye, scent of chamisa,
and now the smell
of thunder, wet basalt,
massive house of spirits
breathing the walls,
walking the earth
in twilight,
beneficent or not,
and you get a whiff
from miles below,
something lithic
stirring in darkness,
waiting.
We live in the rift.
And what can we do
but sit down at the table
and pass the platters,
eating and drinking
this world, our
brief time together
slipping into
rhythms of water
pouring south
under cottonwood,
their great antlers,
spreading tines,
winged seeds
waiting on the wind,
on songlines

in the leaves,
river-throat
laying down
its thudding beat,
and plumed children
tear loose, and fly.

Bone Box

When you are finally finished with the manuscript of what even in your best moments you barely believe is poetry, you give it a name: Bone Box. And then you give yourself a name. You've been hiding forever and this pile of papers blows your cover. The name Danielle Clausen comes to mind, not random, you saw it in the paper, her body discovered in the alley off California Street.

Not a sinister place in daylight. An umbrella tree, wedged between the asphalt and cinderblock wall of the Bombay Inn, juts its trunk out at an odd angle. There's no room for a tree, but it keeps spreading its Asian leaves. The tree managed to grow where no one wanted it. After a girl is dead, they print her name and what she suffered, she's only a body. Danielle was young.

But you do tell a friend you've made this thing that could be a book and you have another name, you're calling yourself Danielle. And she laughs. Now I know, she says. What? Now I know your fantasies. Danielle. A sexy French name. Bubble baths. Carafes. Chocolate. No, no, no, you explain, the name is a metaphor. Gradually, you realize how far off you are, and your voice peters out.

After being close all these years, you've lost your words. It hits you: a dead girl doesn't get up from the pavement. She stays empty. Chalk outline and empty asphalt. She's the low water pressure on the ninth floor of the Hotel Cecil. She's the last words spoken: *Do you like it? Looks like you do.* Your friend tells you, I'm sorry, it's like you're spreading murder over everything.

And should you explain your life as a girl, a gash, a tree with nerve clouds for leaves, your life as a coyote loping across Bristol Road headed for the barranca, a scavenger lapping black birdsong. Your life as a socket, the bulbs forming a line, as a doorpost, a pinhole, a thimble, a shadow, as a slab of meat—we tear our own flesh, Danielle, what is our food?

You're a mantle in a Coleman lantern—a match touches the cloud, fire gasps and rises. On the edge of wider conflagration. You could flare at any moment but the little net of fire holds, so far the filigree is holding, and the precipitate is water.

To go on living a tree like that finds its way beneath concrete, taps into something, maybe a leaky pipe. Say it: to be vascular lace, to reach upward, to be water torn apart by light, to make sugar, to make sugar, to live.

And when damage closes your ears there's still a sound you hear, dense, as of tissue or layers of flesh, I think it's the tissue of life, Danielle, and the sound is like running water.

XXX

Mad Meg

Suppose anger is a habitation: one day the walls go plum red, crackle into flame. You rush out and a thousand other women are stepping through fiery doorjambs. It happened that way. Our bones formed a burning village. Our bones said coruscate. Our bones said gorgeous. We'd eaten dust for years. Never knew how explosive it was.

All I said was, I'm so hungry, I could gut a house. The women sprang up behind me like a battalion of excellent witches. They shouted: Are you tired of feeling for all of Flanders? When I screamed *yes,* the column began to march.

Most of my questions are giants themselves. The doctors blamed me for mystery glands, ropy webs of blood. By then, my body had grown a great bosom a hot volume. Glands are secrets never to be discussed. Burgeoning is not innocent.

I didn't want to be a girl, so I made myself into a ship, a mass of confused rigging. A full moon hung over the crow's nest. I dyed my hair black. The knife was an ordinary kitchen implement roped to my waist. Used to crack the breastbone of countless cockerels. I pressed the frog creatures to my own amphibious breasts.

Northern Lights and Sound

They said it was synesthesia, they said it was only
human, no sound, they said, *what folklore*. . . . But
it goes on ticking, this question of silence, of
what's coming in on the solar wind (wind flowers?)
Is it possible to hear dreams that stream through
the night sky at certain latitudes—*yes*, I say, they're
magnetically charged like ghosts, everyday camp
fires, any room you walk into. Have you ever
gone nocturnal, gone so far north that day never
dawns? In those latitudes, the idea is we know nothing
about depth, don't know what we can't see, it's dark
inside our bodies. When the auroras sing their hissing
songs, pianissimo sparks and clicks, claps and slaps
when air cracks open, when night swirls her ruffled
skirts, her cloak of many colors, is it the music
you'd choose? Maybe not, but why choose—why not
let color be sound, be stain, be scrim, why not ask
who ground the yarrow for ochre, brewed the spell
to bind dark to light, painted the walls in this, our
labyrinth. Storm is of the essence. The dancer's
under the hill—can you see her scarves in the night?

Mapping Hallucinations

It starts as an aura but grows into a walled city
in a lake. Why so small an island prison—two cormorants
can barely spread their wings here—oh, my black
crown, my green legs, my once-upon-a-friend-and-
I-broken-on-the-wheel. Standing tall is counted
as a virtue. Loneliness can be stately, if you ask
a Great Blue, and what a dagger for a mouth.
My sister says 'anger's not a spear, it's a torch,
one end glowing red,' but herons come equipped
with a lance, and a knife, and a pair of scissors.
Why begin enthralled, and end an insufficient
thrall? Once a man asked a girl, *how old are you,*
honey, about twelve, in the jagged light of afternoon—
can you see this girl hitchhiking in the torn air, she's
old enough to be a fortified medieval town—anger
carved every stone in the wall, this girl is hewn.

Space-time Tsunami

If most of the universe is dark energy,
                    why should we be any different?

Pick a wave, any wave—it's just energy in motion,
shock, or plasma, or the wide ocean shrugging
its shoulders when space becomes time
                    and 'time is not at the root of our problem'.

The good ship Charon's anchored offshore, laden
with otter pelts—*soft gold*, they call it.
Our tsunami strikes during the Napoleonic wars,
                    but what's California to Napoleon
that he should weep for her otters?   Nothing.

I had a friend who raked her fingers through my hair, gathered
a hank in a great knot, *Hey, Strange Attractor,* she used to say,

my binary star, my pristine, my flammable—how we orbited,
each to each.
                    I had a friend who convened the dead. When we spoke,
water seemed to leave the beach—the sea scrolling backwards and her,
strolling right out onto newborn land—that reckless.

Hey ferryman, come on over here, ferry, ferry, ferryman . . .

We exist now as thirteen egrets in the canopy of a tree
so far from water that at first they look like
paper lanterns
                    to the observer who has no place to stand

and still I walk on through the great hall of swallows swirling
like Valkyries, like volute, like alley oop,

we do not speak, I'll trail after for a hundred years.

The Country That Doesn't Exist

I still hear the sound of women at night
crossing the cobblestones, filmy kerchiefs
over their hair, the mic mac of their clogs—
this in a country that doesn't exist. But
don't tell that to the storks who flap in from
Africa and build stick houses on battlements.
And consider the swans: laying their warm
breasts down on banks that mark no border.
The Moors passed through this impossible
country once and left behind their longings,
and what can anybody do about that? Or the
oblique solitude of the river sweeping down-
stream forever filling the emptiness of its bed
with more emptiness . . . light spills onto its
flecked back, coriander light, clove light, sesame,
the flower inside my eye opening to receive—
those hungry flowers—if a particle is a prison,
a wave is a ripple inside the wake of a pair
of swans. Whoopers. No, I will not marry again.

Poem on a female goldfinch

Willow-green shy girl
gazing at me
from a tree
of hard green lemons,
wanting something
from this field
where I wait,
my quiet, her courage,
deep green
of the broadleaf—
prosperous weed—
that country squire
who sets the table
of himself
with round-bellied aphids.
She jumps
their swollen curves,
little sap buckets—
yellow, chartreuse, lime,
my goldfinch,
moss green abbess
in the zendo
at meal-time,
her way-deep hunger
koan and blessing.
Fleshpots, earthbeads,
she plunges and gulps,
one eye on
the beholder,
white streak
in my hair,
after all this time
on earth
invited to the feast.

A Grove of Trees

The old women knew the men were police
before I did, waiting
for a bus when Vice surrounded me
all dressed alike,
as though plainclothes had only one meaning,
of course, I wasn't in my skin—
small and tight
like an immature fig,
dense, a little black hole,
when I finally figured
how those men would use me
if they forced me
in their car.
At first, I thought hand over the license
and the cops go away.
I didn't know what else to try.
I wasn't the girl
they were looking for.
Except I was.
The old women saw before I saw,
thick-boned women
with arms of slurry,
women who pulled wire carts home from market
twice a week, all those years after their hearts broke
with the news
from Poland,
old women at eight in the morning
in our poor neighborhood,
already done shopping at Boy's Market,
schlepping their carts
loaded with potatoes and milk
and Weber's Bread.
You can't reason with power.
I didn't know an elderly Jewish man
would cross the perimeter,
walk right into the interrogation,
he didn't have time

to lift his mechanical
voice box
to the hole in his neck
and no time to speak
before they struck him in the chest.
He staggered back
still trying to raise his buzzing machine.
I didn't know
what the grandmothers intended
in the wide morning light,
after the bones and bulldozers and years of grief—
they formed a grove
around us
and did not speak—
this is how grandmothers muster,
silence, iron eyes,
not one leaf moving,
this is how they meet force—
light came stronger, they waited in silence.
I held still
and did not look,
forbidden to see their faces,
forbidden to gaze on the LAPD,
because looks can tilt
shame to rage.
The old women called
on heart wires
we are your mothers too,
and they were large, a grove of trees,
the quiet from the leaves
flowing onto street corners
onto the little knot
of cops, the girl,
the edges of the leaves disappearing
into light,
they never said a word,
but everything I needed to know

waited in their silence—
it took decades
to decipher—
grandmothers built a door with their mind,
and then they helped me
through it,
I heard inside my body
Daughter, get on the bus
and the light was blue
and the air was chill
and the bus rolled up
and the door swung open.

Rough Innocence

Young pine twenty feet tall—
too close to a mature sycamore,
                                    spindly little pine,
                rough innocence and augury,
        too close to the smooth mottled trunk
                                    the graceful arms.

Five years of drought
and your lower branches almost bare,
                                    a few fountains of sallow
and rust, and still you reach   bending your nature
bending near the tip
                above the sycamore limb.

                                    This morning
great-bellied clouds drift
                against the mountains,
                        caravels of light
        and shadow.

                                    Early December
four days after rain—
                already bouquets of needle-green
rise out of gray.
                                    A hundred feet away
San Isidro Creek slides into being,
                        darkens its boulders
rushing off,
                going where water goes.

My palm against your knobbed trunk—

                here you are, Survivor.

Portion

I see we're not so different
from blackberry briars crouched

beneath the force of wind—
how small they make themselves—

we must curve our bodies
and bend our faces low.

Coyote brush is holding on,
the broom is reaching

down the headland, waves
heave portions of infinity.

Here's fennel for opening
the throat, and blue-eyed

grass for endings.
Look now, twilight,

and that cloud overhead
streaming west,

a kind of helix, laddered
and spiraled, life

ascending and descending.
Someday we'll travel there.

To the Grandmothers

Chernobyl, thirty years later

Old women with side gardens and jars
of moonshine alone in empty villages,

tell me, solitary lynx, multitudinous wolf
pack, how do you do it—all my life I've lived

in cities, bought food from grocery stores—
what's it like to return to the abandoned zone

on foot, reclaim your cottage beside the dank
canal, to howl, to hunt in packs, to foal calves,

fell trees, light down in the bodies of swans
and swim in cooling ponds, why would you

fly three thousand miles to build a nest
inside the cracked concrete sarcophagus

over the remains of reactor four? She grins,
hands over a jelly jar of vodka, the good stuff,

Motherland is motherland, she says.

ACKNOWLEDGMENTS

Sincere thanks is given to the editors of the following journals for first publishing some of the poems, sometimes in different versions, in this book:

Apercus Quarterly: "Lament" and "Self-Portrait as Daphne"; *Bosque*: "Gray Fox" and "For the Poet Enheduanna"; *Guttural* (London): "Interrogation"; *Kenyon Review*: "The Understory" and "A Grove of Trees"; *Levure Litteraire*: "Two for a Penny" and "Night Traveling"; *Miramar*: "Star Pine"; *The New Yorker*: "A Natural History of Light" and "The Country That Doesn't Exist"; *San Pedro River Review*: "Speaking to My Father on War"; *Slant*: "I Still Say Your Name"; *Solo Novo*: "Keats at Fourteen" and "No, She Didn't Think the Road Was Dangerous"; *Spillway*: "Poem beginning in loneliness," "Ode to Apples," "To the Grandmothers," and "Rough Innocence."

To my husband, Phil Taggart, for his untiring support and assistance, my love *por vida*; to Nereyda de la O, you are my inspiration. Gratitude and love to my crazy, darling family. Thank you, Janet and Nancy, for all your completely necessary support. Heartfelt thanks always to New Issues Press, to the Vermont College community of writers, especially my teachers, Nancy Eimers, Cynthia Huntington, William Olsen, Betsy Sholl, and David Wojahn, for your example and brilliance. Many thanks to BOA Editions and Peter Conners, Jenna Fisher, and Melissa Hall. Deep gratitude to Ed Ochester and the tireless folks at the University of Pittsburgh Press's Pitt Poetry Series, and to friends in the poetry community who sustain one another and have sustained me: Amy Uyematsu, Suzanne Lummis, David St. John, Susan Terris, Mifanwy Kaiser, Kim Young, Enid Osborn, John Brantingham, Lee Rossi, Joy Manesiotis, Holaday Mason, Sarah Maclay, Mary Anne McFadden, Sandra Hunter, Dorothy Barresi, Lauren Henley and Jonathan Maule, Mariano Zaro, Ines Monguio, Christopher Buckley, Dian Sousa, Richard Beban and Kaaren Kitchell, Mary Kay Rummel, Oneita Hirata, Jim Natal and Tania Baban, Paula C. Lowe, Patty Seyburn, Lynne Thompson, Candace Pearson, Jim Cushing, Kevin Clark, the Salon at Gaby's, Summer Women, Bookish Ladies, and the venerable Sunday Poets: Glenna Luschei, Bruce Schmidt, David Starkey, Chryss Yost, Paul Willis, Perie Longo, and John Ridland. You're always in my heart, Jackson Wheeler and Lee McCarthy. Lynda Hull, *te recuerdo*. Laure-Anne Bosselaar, you are a gift in my life.